Visual World

العالم المصور

The
Majestic
Qur'an

50+ Inspiring Colouring Activities to Discover Allahs' Divine Message & Wisdom

Mosaic Tree Press

ISBN 978-1-916524-64-4

All artwork was designed and licensed by Freepik.com

First printing, 2023

Published by Mosaic Tree Press
Browse our complete catalogue of publications at MosaicTree.org

Published by
Mosaic Tree Press

بسم الله الرحمن الرحيم

In the name of God, the Most Gracious, the Most Merciful

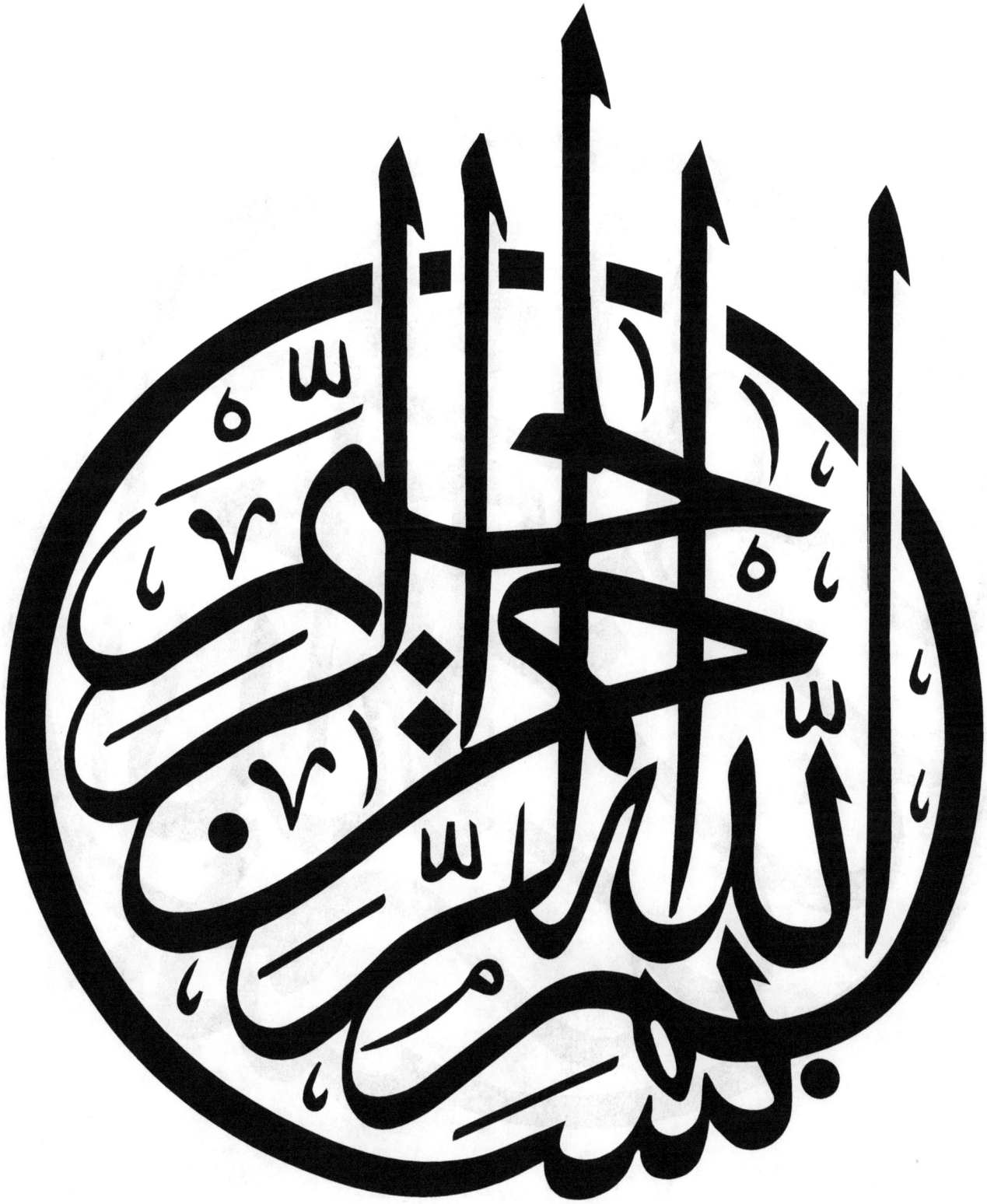

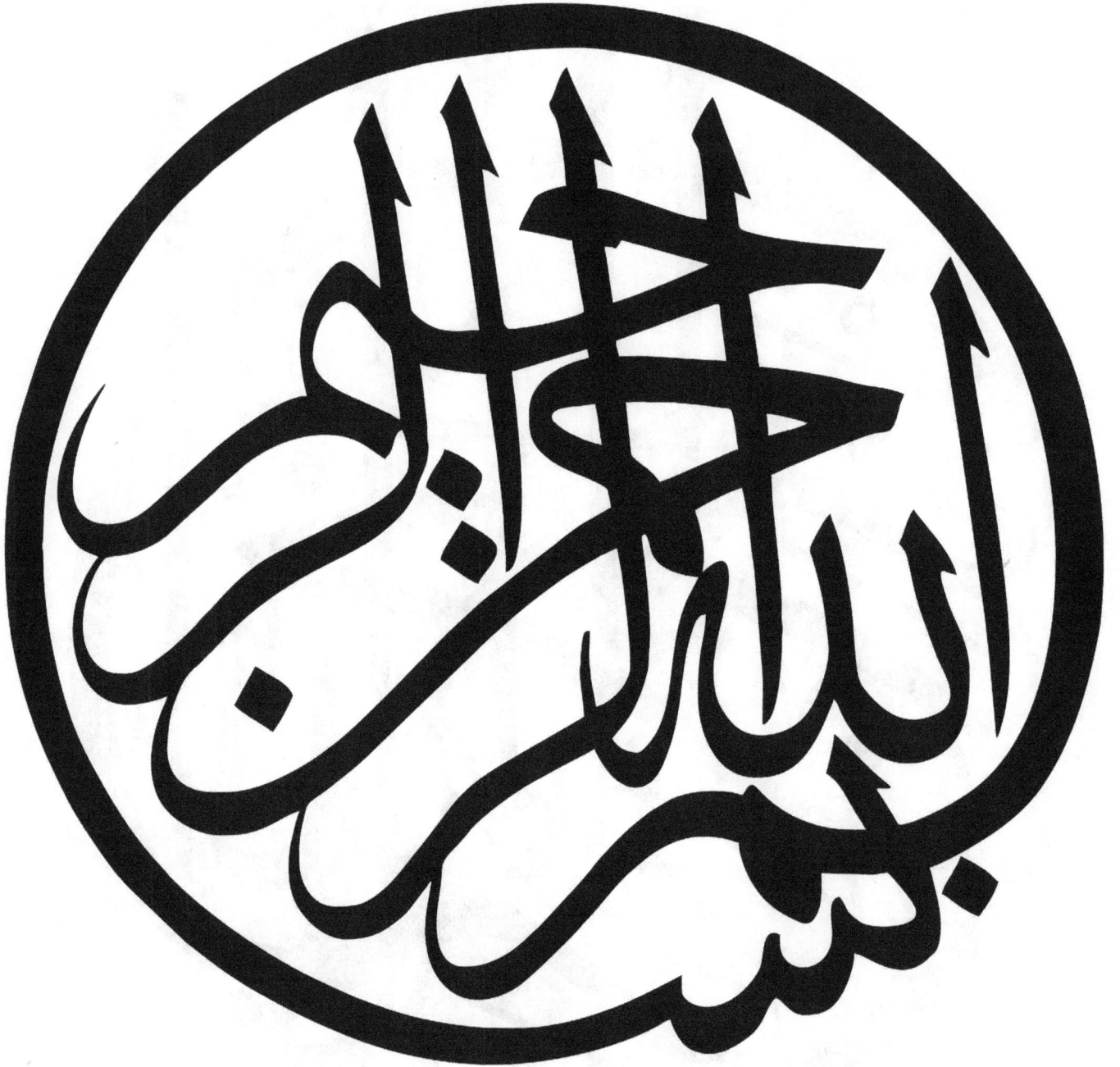

بِسْمِ اللَّهِ الرَّحْمَٰنِ الرَّحِيمِ

بسم الله

القرآن الكريم

القرآن الكريم

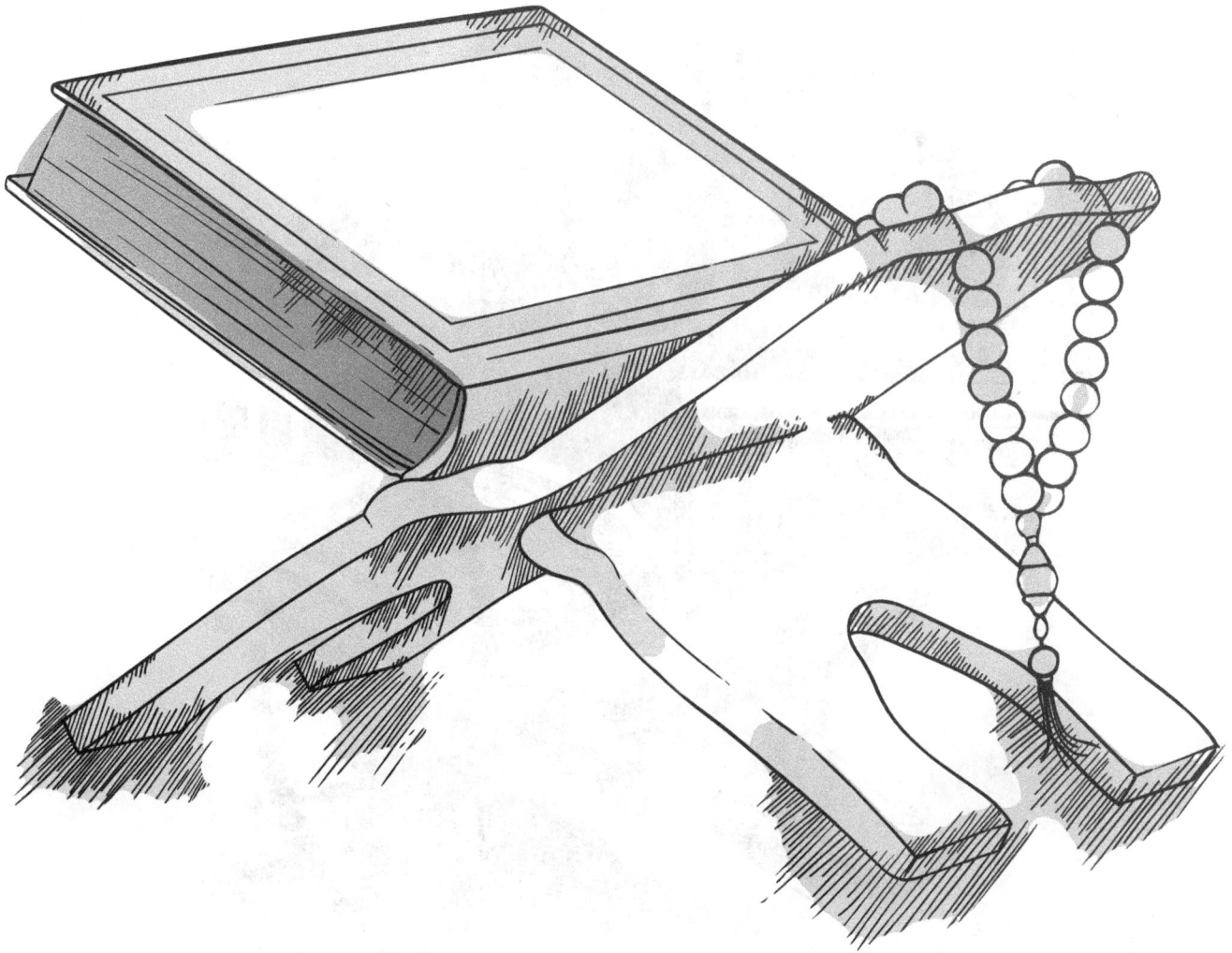

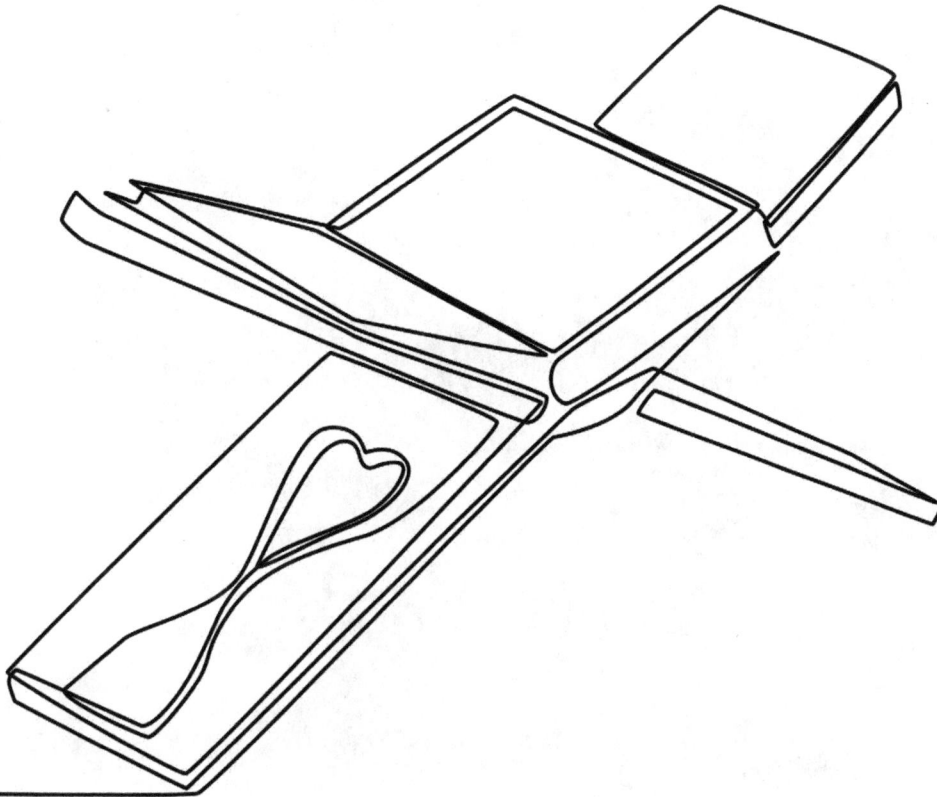

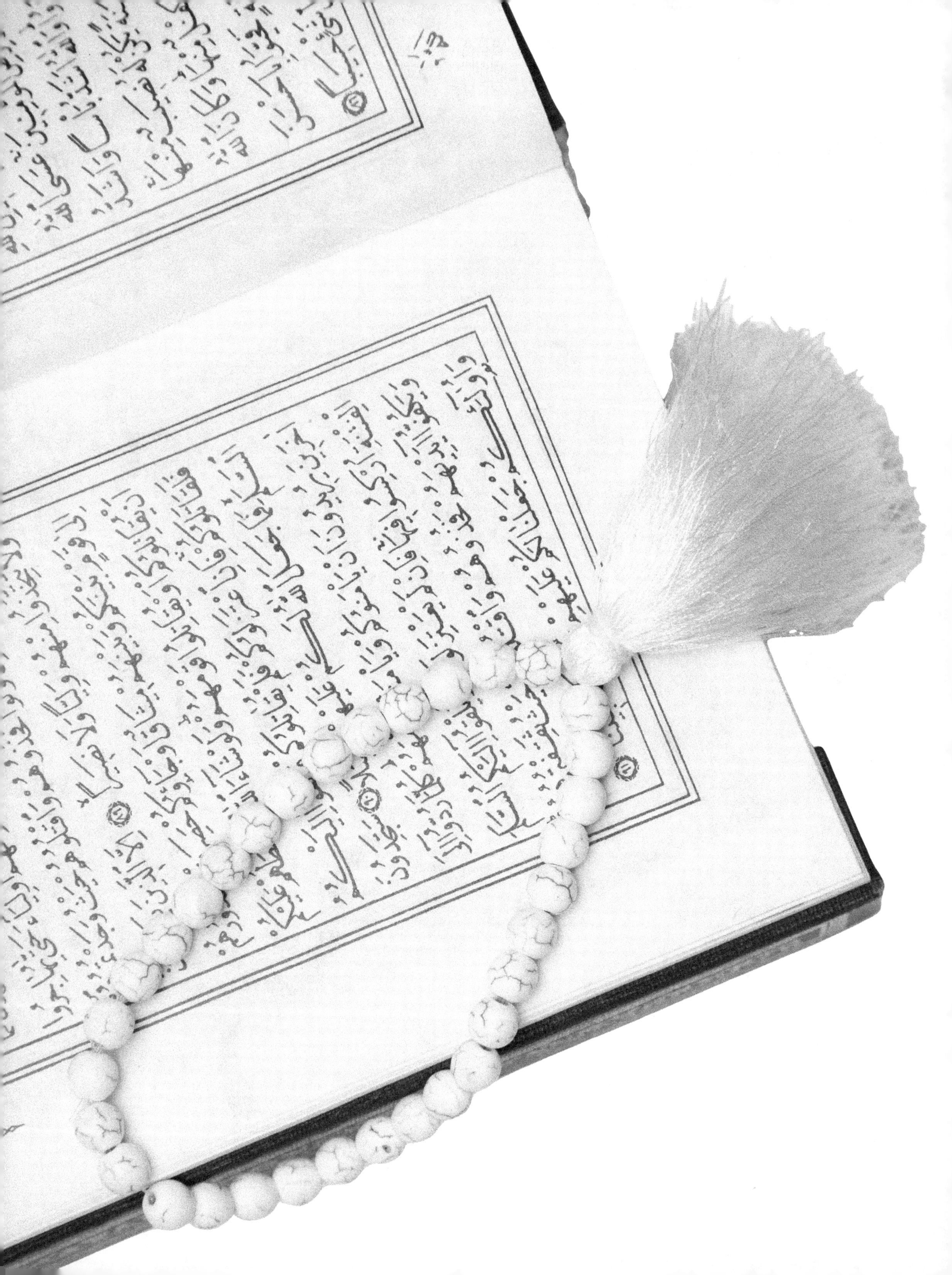

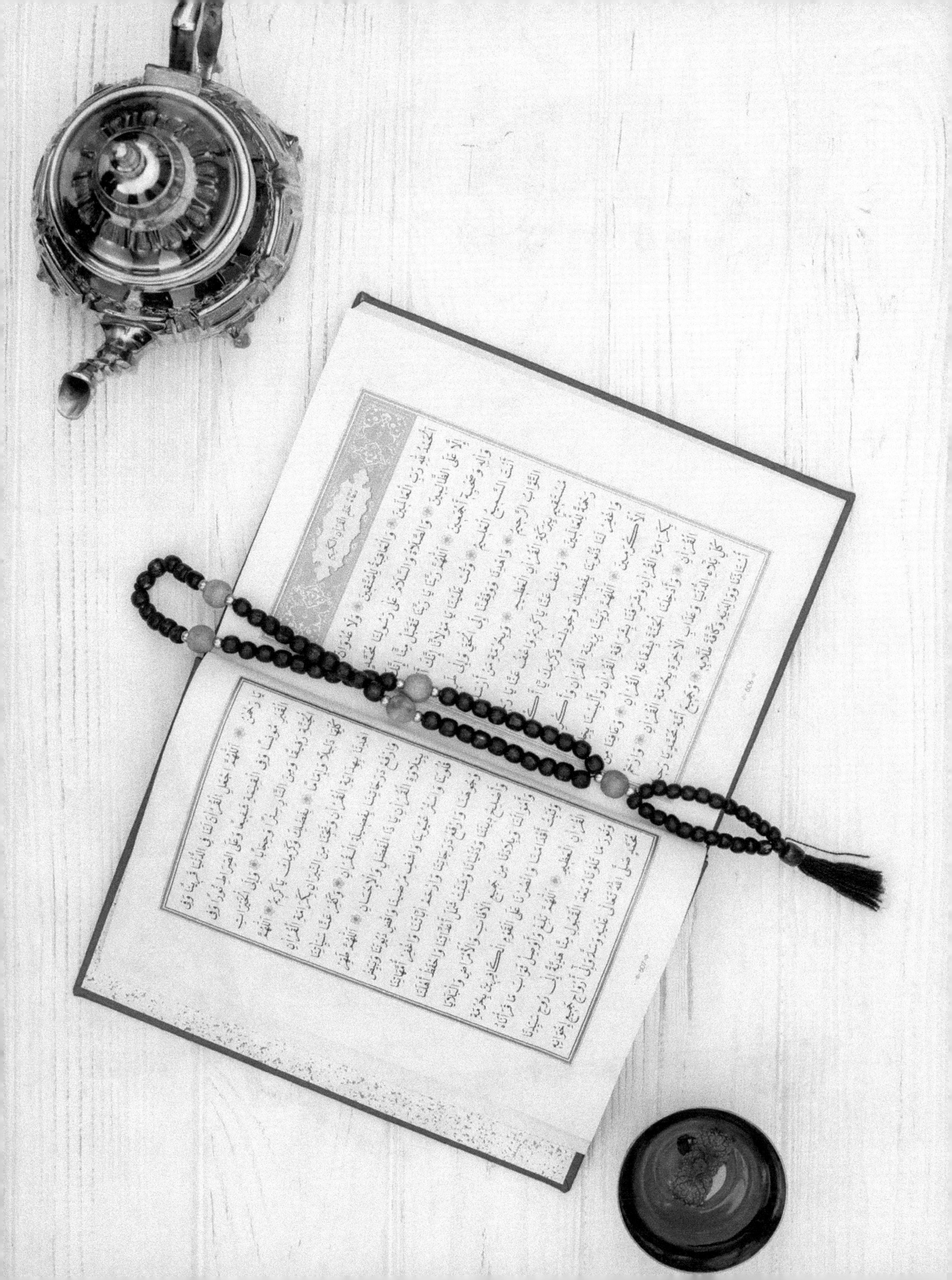

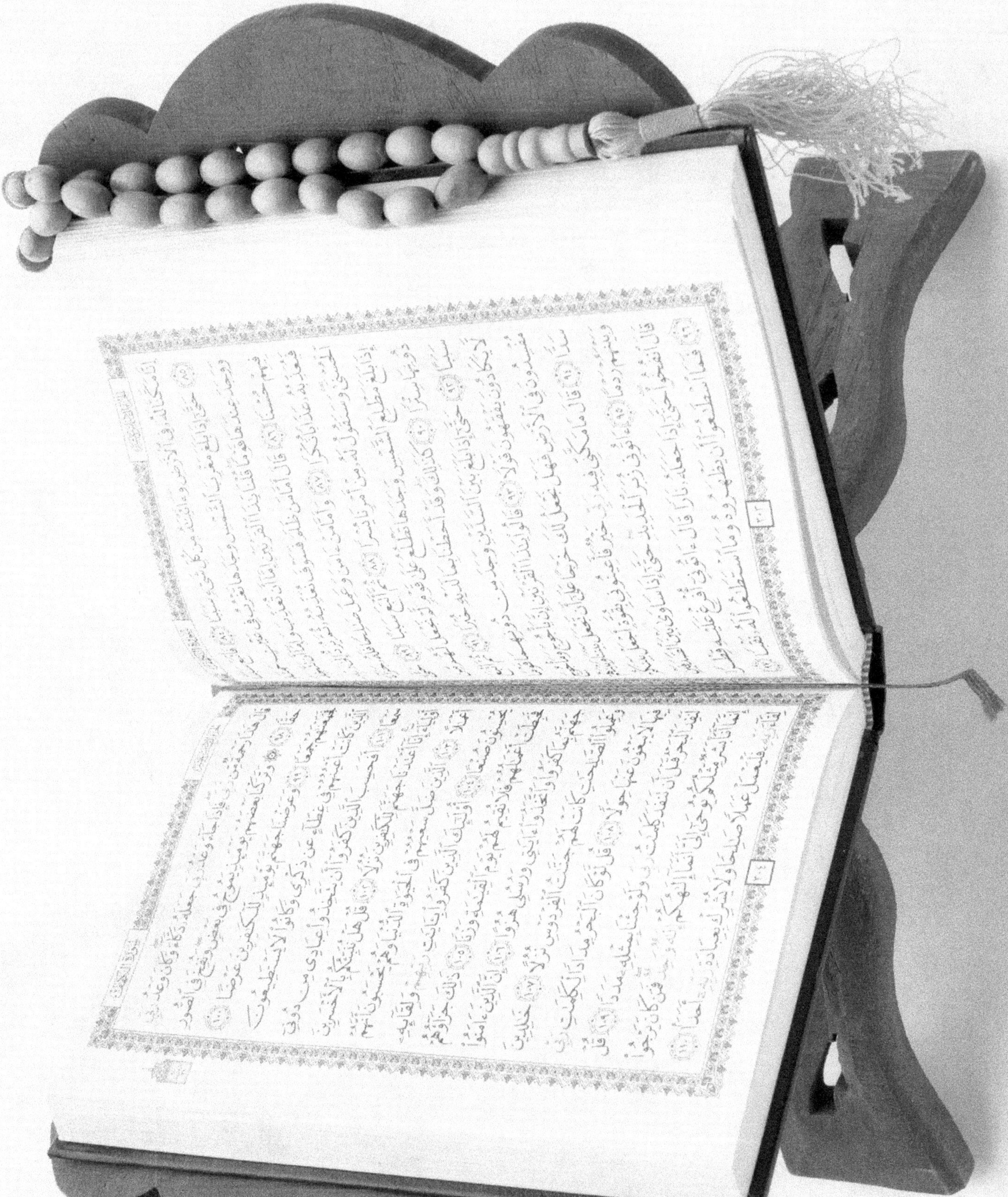

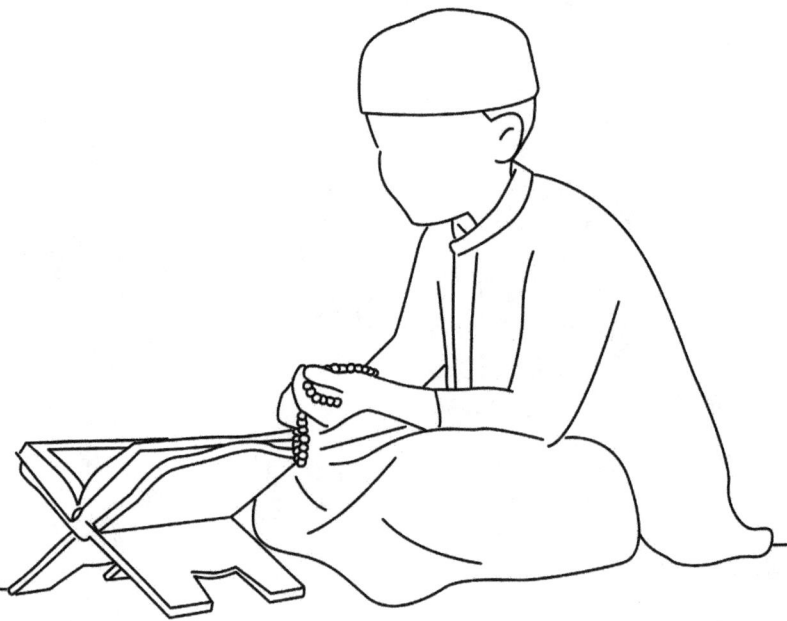

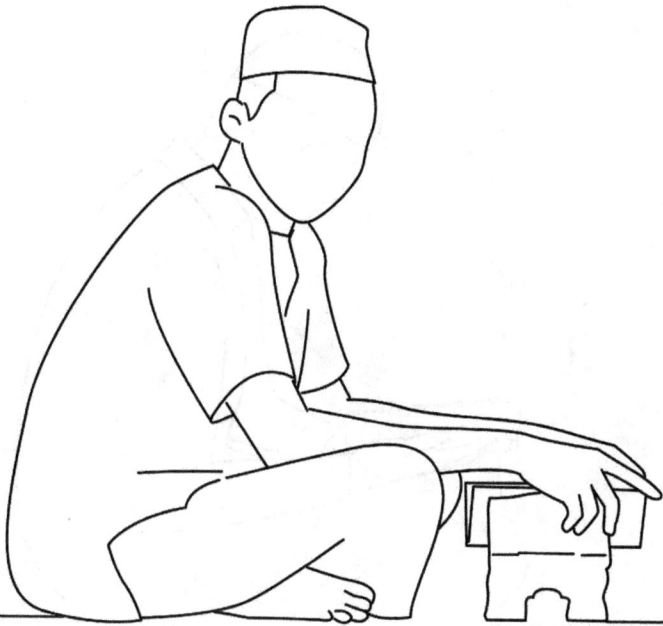

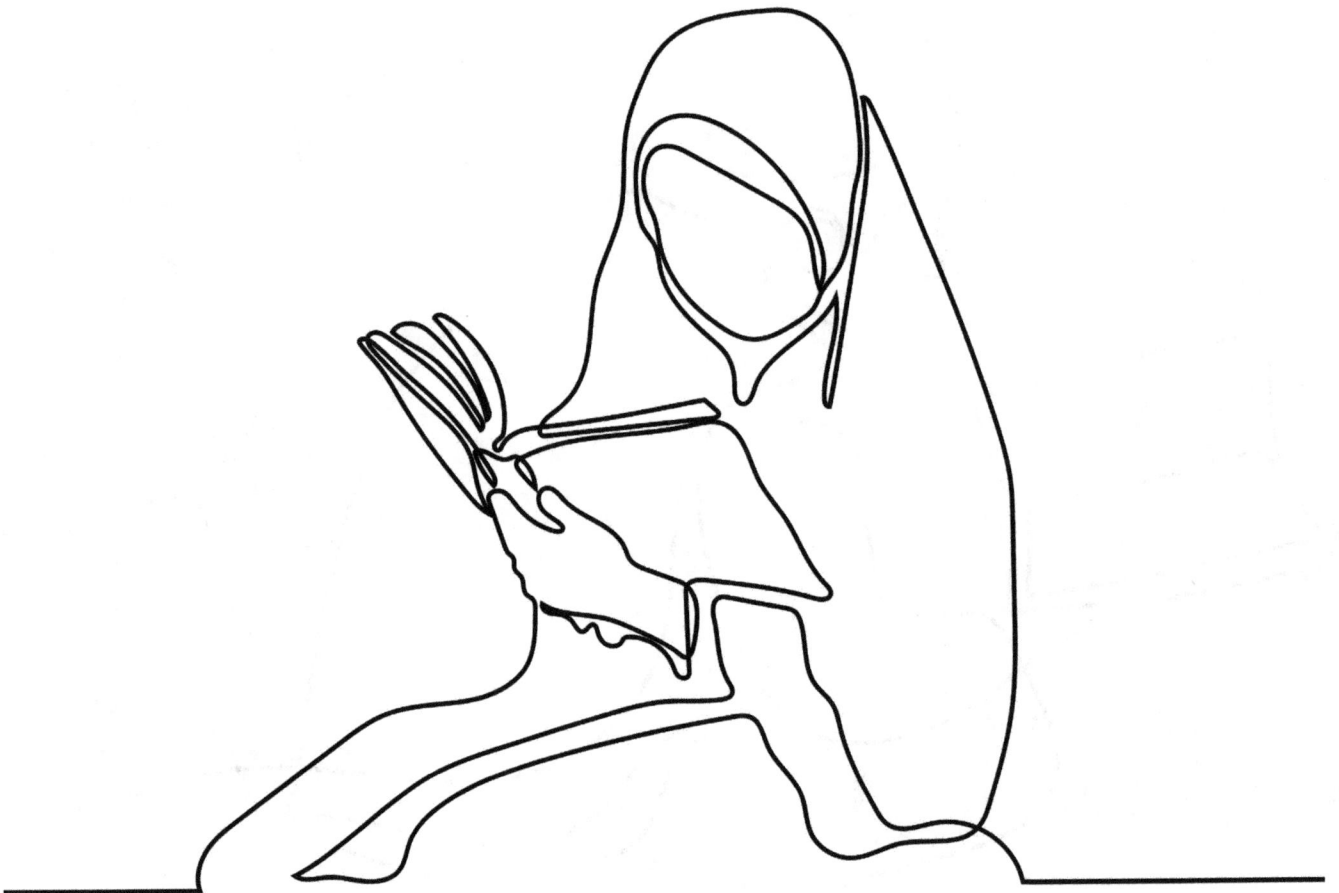

وَقُل رَّبِّ زِدْنِي عِلْمًا

"My Lord, increase me in knowledge" —
— The Noble Qur'an, Taha, 20:114

لا مَلْجَأَ مِنَ اللَّهِ إِلَّا إِلَيْهِ

There was no refuge from Allah except in Him
— **The Noble Qur'an, At-Tawbah 9:118**

وَمَا أَرْسَلْنَاكَ إِلَّا رَحْمَةً لِّلْعَالَمِينَ

We have sent you ˹O Prophet˺ only as a mercy
for the whole world.
— **The Noble Qur'an, Al-Anbya 21:107**

"And be humble with them out of mercy, and pray"
— The Noble Qur'an, Al-Isra, 17:24

لا حول ولا قوة إلا بالله

THERE IS NO POWER
NOR MIGHT SAVE IN ALLAH

There is no power or might except with Allah
— **The "Hawqala" Phrase**

بِسْمِ اللَّهِ الرَّحْمَٰنِ الرَّحِيمِ

اللَّهُ لَا إِلَٰهَ إِلَّا هُوَ الْحَيُّ الْقَيُّومُ لَا تَأْخُذُهُ سِنَةٌ وَلَا نَوْمٌ لَّهُ مَا فِي السَّمَاوَاتِ وَمَا فِي الْأَرْضِ مَن ذَا الَّذِي يَشْفَعُ عِندَهُ إِلَّا بِإِذْنِهِ يَعْلَمُ مَا بَيْنَ أَيْدِيهِمْ وَمَا خَلْفَهُمْ وَلَا يُحِيطُونَ بِشَيْءٍ مِّنْ عِلْمِهِ إِلَّا بِمَا شَاءَ وَسِعَ كُرْسِيُّهُ السَّمَاوَاتِ وَالْأَرْضَ وَلَا يَئُودُهُ حِفْظُهُمَا وَهُوَ الْعَلِيُّ الْعَظِيمُ

The Throne Verse (ٱلْكُرِسِيِّ, Ayat Al-Kursi)
— **The Noble Qur'an 2:255**

بسم الله الرحمن الرحيم

قل هو الله أحد الله الصمد لم يلد ولم يولد ولم يكن له كفوا أحد

Say: He is Allah, the One and Only;
Allah, the Eternal, Absolute;
He begetteth not, nor is He begotten;
And there is none like unto Him.
— **The Noble Qur'an, Al-Ikhlas, 112-1-4**

سُورَةُ النَّاسِ

Say, "I seek refuge in the Lord of mankind,
The Sovereign of mankind.
The God of mankind,
From the evil of the retreating whisperer
Who whispers [evil] into the breasts of mankind
From among the jinn and mankind."
— The Noble Qur'an, An-Nas, 114 1-6

"Be!" And it is"
— The Noble Qur'an, Ghafir 40:68

"I seek refuge in Allah from the accursed satan (devil)."

أَعُوذُ بِاللهِ مِنَ الشَّيْطَانِ الرَّجِيمِ

"And hold firmly together to the rope of Allah"
— The Noble Qur'an, Ali 'Imran 3:103

قل هو الله أحد الله الصمد لم يلد ولم يولد ولم يكن له كفوا أحد

Say: He is Allah, the One and Only;
Allah, the Eternal, Absolute;
He begetteth not, nor is He begotten;
And there is none like unto Him.
— The Noble Qur'an, Al-Ikhlas, 112-1-4

"Call upon Me, I will respond to you."
— **The Noble Qur'an Ghafir 40:60**

"So seek your Lord's forgiveness and turn to Him in repentance. Surely my Lord is Most Merciful, All-Loving."

— **The Noble Qur'an, Hud, 11:90**

Say: He is Allah, the One and Only;
Allah, the Eternal, Absolute;
He begetteth not, nor is He begotten;
And there is none like unto Him.
— The Noble Qur'an, Al-Ikhlas, 112-1-4

Publications by Mosaic Tree Press

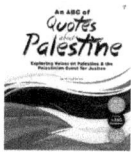

An ABC of Quotes About Palestine: Exploring Voices on Palestine & the Palestinian Quest for Justice (2023)

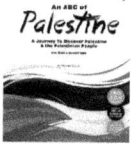

An Abc of Palestine: A Journey To Discover Palestine & The Palestinian People For Kids & Grown Ups (2023)

Palestine: 200+ Cut-Out & Collage Images for Arts & Crafts Activities (2023)

Palestine: 50+ Colouring Activities to Celebrate Palestine & the Palestinian People (2023)

My Journey Through The Most Beautiful Names of Allah: Arabic Reader & Activity Book for Kids: **(Volume 1, 2 & 3)** (2023)

My First Arabic Alphabet & Colouring Book [Arabic for Little Ones] (2023)

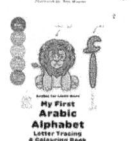

My First Arabic Alphabet: Letter Tracing & Colouring Book [Arabic for Little Ones] (2023)

Essential Arabic Readers: Alphabet Letters with Vowels & Pronunciation Symbols, Mosaic Tree Press (2022)

Similar Sounding Letters in Arabic: Essential Arabic Readers (2023)

Essential Arabic Readers: Arabic Alphabet Writing Practice Handbook, Mosaic Tree Press (2023)

Listen, Read & Write: Arabic Alphabet Letter Groups [Essential Arabic Readers] (2023)

My First Arabic Numbers Reader & Colouring Book, Mosaic Tree Press (2023)

My First Arabic Colours: Reader & Activity Book for Kids, Mosaic Tree Press (2023)

My Arabic Animal Alphabet Reader, Arabic for Little Ones, Mosaic Tree Press (2023)

My First Arabic Alphabet Reader [Arabic for Little Ones] (2023)

My Arabic Learning Journals: My Abc Dictionary (English-Arabic), Mosaic Tree Press (2022)

My Arabic Learning Journals: My Abc Dictionary (Arabic- English), Mosaic Tree Press (2022)

My Arabic Learning Journals: Thematic Vocabulary, Mosaic Tree Press (2022)

I Am .... An ABC of Empowering Self-Affirmations: A Guided Journal for Self-Discovery, Self-Growth & Resilience (2022)

My Journey through Ramadan & Eid Al-Fitr (Arabic for Little Ones), Mosaic Tree Press (2023)

CoronaVirus Lexicon: A Practical Guide for Arabic Learners & Translators (M. Diouri & M. Aboelezz 2023)

Arabic & Islamic Mosaic & Calligraphy Colouring Journal (Volume 1: Islamic Quotes) (2022)

Browse our full catalogue at

MosaicTree.org

Arabic Script & Sounds

Arabic Vocabulary

Arabic for Little Ones

Arabic/Islamic Mosaic & Calligraphy

Arabic Learning Journals

Well-Being & Character Development

Mosaic Tree Press
MosaicTree.org

بحمد الله

Completed with the grace of God